W9-CAJ-539

-am as in ham

Mary Elizabeth Salzmann

Consulting Editor Monica Marx, M.A./Reading Specialist

ABDO Publishing Company

Published by SandCastle™, an imprint of ABDO Publishing Company, 4940 Viking Drive, Edina, Minnesota 55435.

Printed in the United States.

Credits
Edited by: Pam Price
Curriculum Coordinator: Nancy Tuminelly
Cover and Interior Design and Production: Mighty Media
Photo Credits: Brand X Pictures, Comstock, Digital Vision, Kelly Doudna, Eyewire Images, Hemera, Image 100, Donna Day/Image State, PhotoDisc, Rubberball Productions, Stockbyte

Library of Congress Cataloging-in-Publication Data

Salzmann, Mary Elizabeth, 1968-
      -Am as in ham / Mary Elizabeth Salzmann.
         p. cm. -- (Word families. Set I)
      Summary: Introduces, in brief text and illustrations, the use of the letter combination "am" in such words as "ham," "clam," "jam," and "dam."
      ISBN 1-59197-223-X
      1. Readers (Primary) [1. Vocabulary. 2. Reading.] I. Title.

PE1119 .S2342144 2003
428.1--dc21   2002037912

SandCastle™ books are created by a professional team of educators, reading specialists, and content developers around five essential components that include phonemic awareness, phonics, vocabulary, text comprehension, and fluency. All books are written, reviewed, and leveled for guided reading, early intervention reading, and Accelerated Reader® programs and designed for use in shared, guided, and independent reading and writing activities to support a balanced approach to literacy instruction.

Let Us Know

After reading the book, SandCastle would like you to tell us your stories about reading. What is your favorite page? Was there something hard that you needed help with? Share the ups and downs of learning to read. We want to hear from you! To get posted on the ABDO Publishing Company Web site, send us e-mail at:

sandcastle@abdopub.com

SandCastle Level: Transitional

-am Words

clam

dam

ham

jam

ram

yam

Faith is going to dig up a clam.

The river is blocked by the dam.

Gena has an apple
and a ham sandwich.

Emma spreads the jam.

The ram walks in the snow.

One yam fell out of the basket.

The Lost Ham

Poor Pam lost her ham.

She thought
she saw it
in a pram.

But it was only baby Sam!

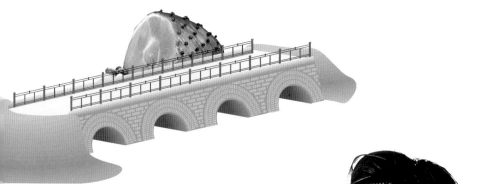

Gram said
she saw it
behind a dam.

But it was just a woolly ram!

Cam said he saw it
in a clam.

But it turned out
to be a yam!

Officer Fram
said he saw it
under a tam.

But it was just
a can of Spam®!

Pam never did find her ham.

So she just ate
some bread and jam.

The -am Word Family

Cam	Pam
clam	pram
dam	ram
Gram	Sam
ham	Spam®
jam	tam
Officer Fram	yam

Glossary

Some of the words in this list may have more than one meaning. The meaning listed here reflects the way the word is used in the book.

clam	a shellfish with two shells hinged together
dam	a barrier built to hold back water
pram	a baby carriage
ram	a male sheep
Spam®	a brand of canned meat
tam	a Scottish wool hat
yam	another name for sweet potato

About SandCastle™

A professional team of educators, reading specialists, and content developers created the SandCastle™ series to support young readers as they develop reading skills and strategies and increase their general knowledge. The SandCastle™ series has four levels that correspond to early literacy development in young children. The levels are provided to help teachers and parents select the appropriate books for young readers.

Emerging Readers
(no flags)

Beginning Readers
(1 flag)

Transitional Readers
(2 flags)

Fluent Readers
(3 flags)

These levels are meant only as a guide. All levels are subject to change.

To see a complete list of SandCastle™ books and other nonfiction titles from ABDO Publishing Company, visit **www.abdopub.com** or contact us at:

4940 Viking Drive, Edina, Minnesota 55435 • 1-800-800-1312 • fax: 1-952-831-1632